JONAH

JONAH

God's Steadfast Love Endures

ANGELA LEE

Contents

Table of Contents

A Plan for This Study

This study is based on the Observation, Interpretation, Application method of Bible study. Each lesson's questions and commentary are designed to help you move through these steps:

Observation: What does the text say?

Read the entire text for comprehension.

Read again and consider: Who was this written to? What is happening in the passage? When and where did this take place? Why did the author write this?

Mark any key words, repeated phrases, or ideas.

Notice any lists, contrasts, comparisons, or types of imagery used.

Interpretation: What does the text mean?

Consult different translations.

Look up cross-references and consider: What do other parts of the Bible have to say about these ideas?

What would the original hearers have thought?

How does this passage fit into the greater story of the Bible? (Creation-Fall-Redemption-New Creation) [see page 5]

Paraphrase: Rewrite the text in your own words.

Consult reliable commentaries.

Application: How do I apply it to my life?

What does this passage tell us about God?

What does this passage tell you about your sin and your need for a Savior?

Is there a command to obey? Is there a promise to claim?

How might this truth transform my life, prayers, and perspective today?

Seeing Jesus in Jonah

After His resurrection, Jesus gave instructions on how we are to interpret books like Jonah.

> "Then he said to them, 'These are my words that I spoke to you while I was still with you, that everything written about me in the Law of Moses and the Prophets and the Psalms must be fulfilled." Then he opened their minds to understand the Scriptures and said to them, 'Thus it is written, that the Christ should suffer and on the third day rise from the dead, and that repentance for the forgiveness of sins should be proclaimed in his name to all nations, beginning from Jerusalem.'" (Luke 24:44-47)

The second *Interpretation* section of each lesson is designed to move you through these questions:

Does the New Testament quote or allude to this text?

If so, how does the later interpretation shed light on the passage at hand?

Does this text speak directly of Christ?

How do the implications of the Gospel make these commands possible?

Does this text reveal a person, event or object in the Old Testament that points toward Christ?

Is this passage predictive of Christ?

How does this passage show us mankind's need for Christ?

How does this passage reveal God's redemptive nature?

Does the passage reveal a biblical theme that points to Christ?

Does the passage show a promise of God that points us to Christ?

(Akin, 10)

I

Introduction to Jonah

Observation and Interpretation

1. Jonah's time as a prophet is recorded in the book of 2 Kings. Read **2 Kings 14:23-28.** What do you learn about Jonah and the time in which he lived?

²³ In the fifteenth year of Amaziah the son of Joash, king of Judah, Jeroboam the son of Joash, king of Israel, began to reign in Samaria, and he reigned forty-one years. ²⁴ And he did what was evil in the sight of the Lord. He did not depart from all the sins of Jeroboam the son of Nebat, which he made Israel to sin. ²⁵ He restored the border of Israel from Lebo-hamath as far as the Sea of the Arabah, according to the word of the Lord, the God of Israel, which he spoke by his servant Jonah the son of Amittai, the prophet, who was from Gath-hepher. ²⁶ For the Lord saw that the affliction of Israel was very bitter, for there was none left, bond or free, and there was none to help Israel. ²⁷ But the Lord had not said that he would blot out the name of Israel from under heaven, so he saved them by the hand of Jeroboam the son of Joash.

²⁸ Now the rest of the acts of Jeroboam and all that he did, and his

might, how he fought, and how he restored Damascus and Hamath to Judah in Israel, are they not written in the Book of the Chronicles of the Kings of Israel?

Read Jonah 1:1-3 and consider the following questions.

1 Now the word of the Lord came to Jonah the son of Amittai, saying, ² "Arise, go to Nineveh, that great city, and call out against it, for their evil has come up before me." ³ But Jonah rose to flee to Tarshish from the presence of the Lord. He went down to Joppa and found a ship going to Tarshish. So he paid the fare and went down into it, to go with them to Tarshish, away from the presence of the Lord.

2.. Summarize the interaction you see between God and Jonah.

3. In verse 3, what do we learn of Jonah's specific goal in fleeing?

Background of Jonah

Who wrote Jonah?

The writer of Jonah is anonymous. The source is likely Jonah's own telling of the story after his return from Nineveh (ESV Study Bible).

What kind of literature is the book of Jonah?

The book of Jonah is a prophetic narrative. It is a telling of God's word coming to Jonah, and the events and miracles revolving around God and His message through His prophet. Jonah is considered to be a Minor prophet; the term "minor" refers to the length of the book in comparison to other prophetic books.

There are many literary features in Jonah including satire, humor, hyperbole, irony, and double entendre. The book has a repeated use of questions, having great rhetorical power (ESV Study Bible).

Where does Jonah fit in with the whole story of the Bible?

God has pursued and spoken to his people since Genesis. He spoke creation into being, and He had a plan to bless the world with His grace. After the fall, which separated mankind from God (Genesis 3), God promised to rescue his people and dwell with them again. He continued speaking through men he appointed like Noah and Abraham, and God made a covenant with Abraham to bless his family, make them a nation, and provide a place for them (Genesis 12). Abraham's family became the Hebrew nation of Israel. Through many trials and wanderings, including enslavement in Egypt (Exodus 1), God was faithful to rescue His people. But the Israelites' sinful state made it so they couldn't dwell with God or hear His words without mediators. So through Moses, the law and sacrificial system were put in place, and priests were called to intercede for the people (Exodus 19-31).

Later on, judges were appointed to guide them, and at the request of Israel, Kings ruled over them (I Samuel 8). These judges and kings often led the people astray, so God continued to raise up **prophets** who were to **speak** to His people on His behalf. The prophets were to remind Israel of God's covenant with them.

Jonah was a prophet in Israel. He was of the generation after the prophets Elijah and Elisha (1 Kings 17- 2 Kings 2), and he would have been a contemporary of theirs. As a prophet, Jonah's job was to stand in between God and man in order to testify about the truth of God to the world. Prophets spoke of God's promises, commanded repentance, warned of judgement, and foretold future events- often pertaining to God's judgement for sin.

In Jonah's day, the kingdom had been divided into Israel in the North, and Judah in the South. Jonah prophesied to the Northern kingdom during the reign of Jeroboam II in 782-753 B.C. (2 Kings 14:23-29).

Jeroboam, "did evil in the eyes of the Lord." But God had mercy on Israel. During Jeroboam's reign, Jonah prophesied that the borders of Israel would be expanded. By God's providence, this border restoration had been made easier by the weakening of Assyria.

Commentators agree that the original audience of Jonah would know him as a patriot, and one who was proud to do ministry in the province of God's chosen people, Israel (Rediscovering, 12). In Israel, Jonah had a successful and appreciated prophetic ministry.

Where does the story take place?

God called Jonah to go to Nineveh. Nineveh was a capital city of Assyria, a bordering enemy of Israel.

Jonah attempted to flee from a port city in Israel named Joppa. He boarded a ship headed toward Tarshish- a barren place in the West Mediterranean.

Commentary on Jonah 1:1-3

Our story opens with an interaction between God and His prophet Jonah. As it had many times before, God's word came to Jonah. This is a typical way for a prophet's narrative to begin. It was to be a recording of God's message to the people.

But in verse 2, the book of Jonah distinguishes itself from other prophetic books. This time God was calling him to "Arise" and call out the wickedness of Nineveh. Every time before this, God's prophets had been sent to call God's own people, Israel, to repentance. God's people saw themselves as chosen and set apart among the nations; they viewed God's covenant promises as belonging to them alone. Jonah was a proud Hebrew, and had little precedent for the idea of a ministry to this pagan nation. And further, Nineveh was in the heart of Assyria, an enemy of Israel.

Nineveh and the Assyrian Empire's reputation of evil was infamous. They were known for their torture, cruel forms of slavery, violence, greed, and immorality (Nahum 3). Nineveh was an enemy that threatened great harm to Israel. Many commentators have compared Jonah's call to minister to Nineveh to a call to minister to Nazi Germany in the World War II era. Jonah was called to leave his comfortable, successful ministry in Israel and warn the wicked and violent city of Nineveh of God's judgement.

Later in the book (Chapter 4:2), Jonah explained the fear that led to his escape attempt here in Chapter 1. Jonah had seen God's judgement and anger toward sin, but he had seen God's grace and compassion, too. God is just and desires retribution for sin, but if repentance was true, His mercy would move him to relent (Begg, Man Overboard).

So Jonah responded to God's grace and God's word by running away. Jonah attempted to flee as far as he possibly could from his assigned destination. He went in the total opposite direction of Nineveh- not walking to the busy city in the east but sailing on a boat to the middle of nowhere in the west.

Jonah took several steps in pursuing his escape, and his plan appeared to work. He may have thought God was providing a way out after all, but subjective experience, impulses, crafty ideas, and a perceived 'sign' of the provision of a boat in the port should not have been what guided Jonah. God communicates and guides us primarily through His revealed word (Ferguson, 22). His word is what He has given to be "a lamp for our feet and a light for our path"(Psalm 119:105) and Jonah was ignoring it.

Jonah's aim is stated in verse 3; he headed "away from the presence of the Lord." Jonah had better theology than to presume He could escape God's sight, but it seems he tried to escape the calling, ministry, and conviction of God.

God had given Jonah a purpose to testify about God's mercy to the Ninevites. Jonah had a different purpose in mind, and so he rejected God's word.

Themes We Will Focus On

Seeing Jesus Christ in Jonah

After His resurrection, Jesus gave instructions on how we are to interpret books like Jonah.

> "Then he said to them, 'These are my words that I spoke to you while I was still with you, that everything written about me in the Law of Moses and the Prophets and the Psalms must be fulfilled." Then he opened their minds to understand the Scriptures and said to them, 'Thus it is written, that the Christ should suffer and on the third day rise from the dead, and that repentance for the forgiveness of sins should be proclaimed in his name to all nations, beginning from Jerusalem.'" (Luke 24:44-47)

Jesus fulfills all of scripture, including the prophets. Jonah is a story of an imperfect prophet that leaves us yearning for our true, compassionate, and merciful Prophet. Each week, the second lesson of each chapter will be a deep dive in understanding how we see Jesus in the book of Jonah. (There is an additional list of interpretation questions in "A Plan for this Study" for reference.) Jesus is the true and better Jonah through His life, death, and resurrection.

Our Purpose: Proclaiming God's grace and compassion towards us.

Jonah's call as a prophet was to testify of God's character and truth to the world. Through Christ, we have been given a similar calling and purpose. If we have been saved by His grace, we are now called to testify about His grace.

1 Peter puts it beautifully:

"But you are a chosen race, a royal priesthood, a holy nation, a people for his own possession, that you may proclaim the excellencies of him who called you out of darkness into his marvelous light. Once you were not a people, but now you are God's people; once you had not received mercy, but now you have received mercy." 1 Peter 2:9-10

We will see throughout the book that Jonah struggled to live according to God's purpose for him. He held fast to a hope and purpose much less secure: his Israelite heritage, his ministry, his pride, and his own self-righteousness. But as Jonah wrestled with his conflicting ambitions, acting childishly and selfishly, God bent down to meet him with humble and gracious compassion. Through Christ, God pursues us with the same humble compassion that He demonstrated to Jonah. As we apply this book, we will discuss how we might behold God's compassion in Jonah's life and ours, so that we may live a life of proclaiming the grace and compassion of God in Christ.

The Power and Purpose of God's Word

In this study we will consider how Jonah rejects God's word (Chapter 1), recalls and returns to God's word (Chapter 2), receives and preaches God's word (Chapter 3), and wrestles with God's word (Jonah 4).

In the book of Jonah, we will refer to the Old Testament available in his day, and God speaking audibly to Jonah as "God's word." For us, the whole Bible, the Old Testament and the New Testament is God's revealed word.

2 Timothy 3:16-17 says:

> "All Scripture is breathed out by God and profitable for teaching, for reproof, for correction, and for training in righteousness, that the man of God may be competent, equipped for every good work."

God's word proves powerful, sufficient, and profitable throughout every interaction in Jonah. As we study the God of Jonah, we will consider our own hearts, and how we should respond to His revealed word.

Application and Reflection

1. Jonah's drifting from God started with his disobedient response to God's words. He was guided by his impulses and desires.

Today, God's word to us is revealed in the Bible. What guides you when you make decisions? What might you do to form habits that encourage guidance through scripture?

2. Jonah was a prophet called to testify about God's truth and grace. Read **Ephesians 1:3-12** and underline some aspects of a Christian's purpose.

3 Blessed be the God and Father of our Lord Jesus Christ, who has blessed us in Christ with every spiritual blessing in the heavenly places, 4 even as he chose us in him before the foundation of the world, that we should be holy and blameless before him. In love 5 he predestined us[b]

for adoption to himself as sons through Jesus Christ, according to the purpose of his will, [6] to the praise of his glorious grace, with which he has blessed us in the Beloved. [7] In him we have redemption through his blood, the forgiveness of our trespasses, according to the riches of his grace, [8] which he lavished upon us, in all wisdom and insight [9] making known[c] to us the mystery of his will, according to his purpose, which he set forth in Christ[10] as a plan for the fullness of time, to unite all things in him, things in heaven and things on earth.

[11] In him we have obtained an inheritance, having been predestined according to the purpose of him who works all things according to the counsel of his will, [12] so that we who were the first to hope in Christ might be to the praise of his glory.

How is our purpose and identity similar to Jonah's?

3. How can this hope and purpose, as explained in Ephesians, encourage you in your calling to follow Jesus?

2

God's Compassion Pursues

Observation and Interpretation– Jonah 1:3-17

Read **Jonah 1:3-17** and consider the following questions.

³ But Jonah rose to flee to Tarshish from the presence of the Lord. He went down to Joppa and found a ship going to Tarshish. So he paid the fare and went down into it, to go with them to Tarshish, away from the presence of the Lord.

⁴ But the Lord hurled a great wind upon the sea, and there was a mighty tempest on the sea, so that the ship threatened to break up. ⁵ Then the mariners were afraid, and each cried out to his god. And they hurled the cargo that was in the ship into the sea to lighten it for them. But Jonah had gone down into the inner part of the ship and had lain down and was fast asleep. ⁶ So the captain came and said to him, "What do you mean, you sleeper? Arise, call out to your god! Perhaps the god will give a thought to us, that we may not perish."

⁷ And they said to one another, "Come, let us cast lots, that we may know on whose account this evil has come upon us." So they cast lots,

and the lot fell on Jonah. [8] Then they said to him, "Tell us on whose account this evil has come upon us. What is your occupation? And where do you come from? What is your country? And of what people are you?" [9] And he said to them, "I am a Hebrew, and I fear the Lord, the God of heaven, who made the sea and the dry land." [10] Then the men were exceedingly afraid and said to him, "What is this that you have done!" For the men knew that he was fleeing from the presence of the Lord, because he had told them.

[11] Then they said to him, "What shall we do to you, that the sea may quiet down for us?" For the sea grew more and more tempestuous. [12] He said to them, "Pick me up and hurl me into the sea; then the sea will quiet down for you, for I know it is because of me that this great tempest has come upon you." [13] Nevertheless, the men rowed hard to get back to dry land, but they could not, for the sea grew more and more tempestuous against them. [14] Therefore they called out to the Lord, "O Lord, let us not perish for this man's life, and lay not on us innocent blood, for you, O Lord, have done as it pleased you." [15] So they picked up Jonah and hurled him into the sea, and the sea ceased from its raging. [16] Then the men feared the Lord exceedingly, and they offered a sacrifice to the Lord and made vows.

[17] And the Lord appointed a great fish to swallow up Jonah. And Jonah was in the belly of the fish three days and three nights.

1. In the chart below, list God's actions, and Jonah's and the sailors' corresponding actions.

God	Jonah	Sailors

2. How does the sailors' reaction to the events show reverence to God and care for others? How does that contrast with Jonah's actions?

3. In verses 11-13, what do the sailors attempt to do? What is their conclusion and resolution in verses 14-16?

Commentary

Verses 4-6

In response to Jonah's fleeing, God pursued him, and sent a great storm. The mariners on the ship to Tarshish were Phoenician. They were renowned and skillful in many things, and these sailors were very accustomed to storms. (Begg, Man Overboard). But this storm was different. The text says they were "afraid and each cried out to his god." It was unlike any they had seen before, and their previous experience and hard work in navigating storms was not making a difference. Additionally, the storm had the marks of divine intervention. It was powerful enough that mariners assumed that gods were responsible; they cried out to these gods for rescue.

However, the one person on the ship who feared a God actually able to change reality was not crying out. Jonah had gone down to the inner part of the ship to sleep—the NIV translation says he was in a "deep sleep" through this violent storm. How could this be? It is unlikely that Jonah's sleep was a peaceful one. Considering the events, it seems likely that this was a sleep of despair and emotional exhaustion from his desperation to flee his God. Disobedience, guilt, and a hardened heart are tiresome.

So while the pagans worked anxiously to protect the ship and each other, Jonah the prophet slept. This was to the shock of the captain of the ship who cried to Jonah, "What do you mean you sleeper? Arise, call out to your God! Perhaps the god might give a thought to us, that we might not perish." So the pagan leader suggests to Jonah the prophet to do what he had been avoiding, and speak to God. Maybe He would "give thought to them that they may not perish?" The sailors had begun to appeal to the mercy of God.

Verses 7-10

Then they cast lots. Jonah must have known at this point that he was about to be found out. Casting lots was a common practice in this time. It involved two stones, carved in the shape of dice (Begg, "Man Overboard"). There was a lot of confidence placed in this process, and God often used it to intervene and provide guidance. They cast lots to see who was responsible for the storm and "the lot fell on Jonah."

Then the sailors ask a series of questions to try to understand Jonah, to which Jonah responds, "I am a Hebrew, and I fear the Lord God who made the sea and the dry land." Tim Keller notes that in such a short book with few words, the fact that Jonah lists that he is a Hebrew first is significant. Jonah, in recalling the fleeing that he is being disciplined for, was still hanging onto his reputation as a Hebrew. He did not answer their question about his occupation. For, though Jonah was a prophet, he may have been ashamed to admit it under his circumstances. (Rediscovering, 50).

Verses 11-17

Jonah explained to the men that in order to stop the storm, they needed to throw him into the sea. They tried as hard as they could to avoid this. The sailors worked harder and harder to fight against the storm themselves until they finally gave up. Then they called out to God in prayer, and they boldly use His covenant name, "Yahweh." They showed reverence and humility as they acknowledged that God can and will do as He pleases, and they asked for His mercy for throwing His prophet into the sea. When they threw Jonah in, the storm ceased. The sailors "feared the Lord exceedingly" and demonstrated their true, repentant faith with sacrifices and vows. These pagans beheld the power and mercy of the God who "made the sea and dryland."

So though Jonah had fled the presence of God in order to avoid showing God's goodness to the pagans, in God's gracious sovereignty, He used Jonah's disobedience to do just that. Sinclair Ferguson notes, "There are times in our lives when the Lord will employ us in His service despite our disobedience, to demonstrate that the grace, the fruit, and the glory are entirely His." (17) God's compassionate pursuit of sinners will not be thwarted.

In verse 17, He pursues Jonah again. In order to rescue him from the sea, "the Lord appointed a great fish to swallow Jonah. And Jonah was in the belly of the fish for 3 days and 3 nights."

Interpretation: Seeing Christ in Jonah Chapter 1

1. Compare Jonah's calling from God in Jonah 1:1-3 to Christ's calling as stated in **Philippians 2:5-11** and **John 1:1-4, 14**.

5 Have this mind among yourselves, which is yours in Christ Jesus, 6 who, though he was in the form of God, did not count equality with God a thing to be grasped, 7 but emptied himself, by taking the form of a servant, being born in the likeness of men. 8 And being found in human form, he humbled himself by becoming obedient to the point of death, even death on a cross. 9 Therefore God has highly exalted him and bestowed on him the name that is above every name, 10 so that at the name of Jesus every knee should bow, in heaven and on earth and under the earth, 11 and every tongue confess that Jesus Christ is Lord, to the glory of God the Father.

1 In the beginning was the Word, and the Word was with God, and the Word was God. 2 He was in the beginning with God. 3 All things were made through him, and without him was not any thing made that was made. 4 In him was life, and the life was the light of men.

14 And the Word became flesh and dwelt among us, and we have seen his glory, glory as of the only Son from the Father, full of grace and truth.

How does Jonah's call to humility point us to Jesus?

2. What do we learn about the character of God through His actions in chapter 1? How do His actions and words point to His redemptive nature?

3. Reflect on the parallels between Jonah's experience in the storm and Jesus's experience in the storm in **Mark 4:35-41.** What are things you notice about the characters and events?

[35] On that day, when evening had come, he said to them, "Let us go across to the other side." [36] And leaving the crowd, they took him with them in the boat, just as he was. And other boats were with him. [37] And a great windstorm arose, and the waves were breaking into the boat, so that the boat was already filling. [38] But he was in the stern, asleep on the cushion. And they woke him and said to him, "Teacher, do you not care that we are perishing?" [39] And he awoke and rebuked the wind and said to the sea, "Peace! Be still!" And the wind ceased, and there was a great calm. [40] He said to them, "Why are you so afraid? Have you still no faith?" [41] And they were filled with great fear and said to one another, "Who then is this, that even the wind and the sea obey him?"

4. Consider the sailor's conclusion to their failed efforts to stop the storm of judgment in verses 13-16. Read **1 Peter 2:22-25.** Compare the sacrifice of Jesus to the 'sacrifice' of Jonah.

[35] On that day, when evening had come, he said to them, "Let us go across to the other side." [36] And leaving the crowd, they took him with them in the boat, just as he was. And other boats were with him. [37] And a great windstorm arose, and the waves were breaking into the boat, so

that the boat was already filling. ³⁸ But he was in the stern, asleep on the cushion. And they woke him and said to him, "Teacher, do you not care that we are perishing?" ³⁹ And he awoke and rebuked the wind and said to the sea, "Peace! Be still!" And the wind ceased, and there was a great calm. ⁴⁰ He said to them, "Why are you so afraid? Have you still no faith?" ⁴¹ And they were filled with great fear and said to one another, "Who then is this, that even the wind and the sea obey him?"

Prayer/Journal Prompt:

Take some time to thank and praise Jesus that He is...

The faithful and obedient Servant who left heaven to serve and give His life as a ransom for many. (1:1-3)

The true Prophet, who commands the wind and waves and rescues us from the storm of judgement by His sacrifice. (1:13-16)

The One whom through God saves by His sacrifice and gathers people from every nation. (1:16)

Application and Reflection

1. As you reflect on the characters and their various responses to God, how are you like the sailors in the story? How are you like Jonah?

2. In his fleeing, Jonah was concerned for his own comfort, pride, and reputation. How does this same pride often hinder us from our obedience to God's word?

3. Regarding this chapter in Jonah, Charles Spurgeon noted, "Should not the privileges and the honour, which your being a believer has brought to you by divine grace, forbid that you should be a slumberer, inactive, careless, indifferent?"

How can your privileges and purpose in Christ lead you to respond obediently to God's word in difficult circumstances this week?

3

God's Grace Restores

Observation and Interpretation- Jonah 2

Read **Jonah 2** and consider the following questions.

2 Then Jonah prayed to the Lord his God from the belly of the fish,
² saying,
"I called out to the Lord, out of my distress,
and he answered me;
out of the belly of Sheol I cried,
and you heard my voice.
³ For you cast me into the deep,
into the heart of the seas,
and the flood surrounded me;
all your waves and your billows
passed over me.
⁴ Then I said, 'I am driven away
from your sight;
yet I shall again look

upon your holy temple.'
5 The waters closed in over me to take my life;
   the deep surrounded me;
weeds were wrapped about my head
6   at the roots of the mountains.
I went down to the land
   whose bars closed upon me forever;
yet you brought up my life from the pit,
   O Lord my God.
7 When my life was fainting away,
   I remembered the Lord,
and my prayer came to you,
   into your holy temple.
8 Those who pay regard to vain idols
   forsake their hope of steadfast love.
9 But I with the voice of thanksgiving
   will sacrifice to you;
what I have vowed I will pay.
   Salvation belongs to the Lord!"
   10 And the Lord spoke to the fish, and it vomited Jonah out upon the dry land.

1. In Chapter 2, Jonah records his prayer in the belly of the fish. Describe Jonah's condition in verses 1-6.

2. As Jonah concludes in verses 7-9, what is his assessment of his own dependence on God's rescue and mercy?

3. Jonah would have been familiar with the Psalms, and he appears to quote several in this prayer. Read **Psalm 18:4-6, 16-19.** What do you think Jonah was learning about the truth of this Psalm during his experience?

4 The cords of death encompassed me;
the torrents of destruction assailed me;
5 the cords of Sheol entangled me;
the snares of death confronted me.
6 In my distress I called upon the Lord;
to my God I cried for help.
From his temple he heard my voice,
and my cry to him reached his ears.

16 He sent from on high, he took me;
he drew me out of many waters.
17 He rescued me from my strong enemy
and from those who hated me,
for they were too mighty for me.
18 They confronted me in the day of my calamity,
but the Lord was my support.
19 He brought me out into a broad place;
he rescued me, because he delighted in me.

4. What is Jonah's conclusion in verse 9? How might this perspective inform him as he considers his calling to the Ninevites?

Commentary

Jonah had been running from the presence of God, but God's discipline led him to address the things he was avoiding. He knew that his deepest need was the very thing he had been fleeing—so in the belly of the fish, Jonah began to seek the presence of God by returning to prayer and scripture.

Down in the deepest of pits, Jonah relied on his training in God's word. The recording of his prayer has quotes, glimpses, and imagery of several Psalms. (Psalm 18, 40,42, 88) Jonah demonstrated his true faith through his praying scripture in the midst of desperation, echoing the Psalmist's cry, "My soul faints with longing for your salvation, I put my hope in your word." (Psalm 119:81) (Ferguson, 34). He acknowledged his need for mercy and thanked God for the salvation that comes from Him alone.

Verses 1-3

Jonah called out to the Lord from his distress, from "the belly of Sheol." In the Old Testament, Sheol refers to death or the afterlife. Jonah acknowledged that he was near death when he cried out to God. Speaking to God, he says, "For you cast me into the deep, into the heart of the seas...."(3). The sailors were the means God used to throw Jonah into the sea, but he acknowledged that God is the one who ordained this difficulty.

Then Jonah referenced Psalm 42:6-7. This Psalm uses the imagery of "waves and billows" to describe God's powerful judgement of sin. So as he recalled this Psalm, he acknowledged that the waves and billows that surrounded him were the result of God's wrath toward his disobedience. Jonah's rebellion had moved to the forefront of his mind.

Verses 4-6

Here Jonah reflected on the worst part of his condition: he had been "driven away" from God's sight and from His presence. Jonah had previously known the fellowship of God, so the apparent separation from Him was even worse than the reality of his physical condition under the sea. But again, we see evidence of Jonah's faith here. He knew what do when his sin separated him from God. He resolved, "I will look upon your holy temple..."

Jonah knew that at the temple, sin offerings were made by the priests so that God might pass over the sin of the people. (Leviticus 6 and 16). He also knew the promise God had given regarding His temple through Solomon in 1 Kings 8:33-40; that no matter the sin or devastation, God would hear his people if they turned toward Him in repentance and prayer at the temple. So when Jonah had reached the lowest point, "down to the land whose bars closed upon me forever..." God, in response to Jonah's prayer of repentance, brought up his life from the pit.

Verses 7-10

At the end of his prayer, Jonah praised God and summarized his experience. He acknowledged that at the bottom of the ocean, his life was fainting away. When he remembered the Lord, his prayer was heard. God acted and saved Jonah by appointing a whale to rescue him from the sea.

Then Jonah acknowledged, "Those who pay regard to vain idols forsake their hope of steadfast love." Other gods, or "vain idols," offer no hope of steadfast love. But as Jonah turned in prayer and looked toward the temple, he recalled God's merciful rescue of him. He was able to rejoice that his God is one of steadfast love and forgiveness. When Jonah ran, God pursued and rescued him in steadfast love and mercy.

So Jonah declared that he would serve, with thanksgiving, the God of steadfast love. Regarding the vow he once made to serve God, he said "he will pay..." What brought about this change in Jonah's heart? The truth that "Salvation belongs to the Lord..."(9).

Though we will see in the next chapters that Jonah's growth and process toward humility is a slow one, there is evidence in chapter 2 of God's wise and perfect teaching method softening Jonah's heart. God showed Jonah how much he needed mercy and that Jonah could never save himself. He needed to experience this mercy so that he might declare it to the Ninevites. In Jonah's life, in the life of Israel, and the life of the Ninevites... salvation is God's doing. With this new perspective, Jonah resolved that this merciful God is more than worthy of his obedience.

God heard Jonah's prayer, and "spoke to the fish, and it vomited Jonah out upon the dry land."(10)

Interpretation: Seeing Christ in Jonah Chapter 2

1. In the midst of mourning over his sin, verse 4 says Jonah looks toward the temple. Read **Leviticus 16:14-16, 2 Chronicles 6:18-21,** and **Hebrews 9:6-7**. What would Jonah know that would cause him to look there?

¹⁴ And he shall take some of the blood of the bull and sprinkle it with his finger on the front of the mercy seat on the east side, and in front of the mercy seat he shall sprinkle some of the blood with his finger seven times.

¹⁵ "Then he shall kill the goat of the sin offering that is for the people and bring its blood inside the veil and do with its blood as he did with the blood of the bull, sprinkling it over the mercy seat and in front of the mercy seat. ¹⁶ Thus he shall make atonement for the Holy Place, because of the uncleannesses of the people of Israel and because of their transgressions, all their sins. And so he shall do for the tent of meeting, which dwells with them in the midst of their uncleannesses.

¹⁸ "But will God indeed dwell with man on the earth? Behold, heaven and the highest heaven cannot contain you, how much less this house that I have built!¹⁹ Yet have regard to the prayer of your servant and to his plea, O Lord my God, listening to the cry and to the prayer that your servant prays before you, ²⁰ that your eyes may be open day and night toward this house, the place where you have promised to set your name, that you may listen to the prayer that your servant offers toward this place. ²¹ And listen to the pleas of your servant and of your people Israel, when they pray toward this place. And listen from heaven your dwelling place, and when you hear, forgive.

⁶ These preparations having thus been made, the priests go regularly into the first section, performing their ritual duties, ⁷ but into the second only the high priest goes, and he but once a year, and not without taking blood, which he offers for himself and for the unintentional sins of the people.

2. As you reflect on your answer to the previous question, read **Hebrews 9:11-14** and **Hebrews 10:19-23.** What is a Christian's hope in mourning over sin?

¹¹ But when Christ appeared as a high priest of the good things that have come, then through the greater and more perfect tent (not made with hands, that is, not of this creation) ¹² he entered once for all into the holy places, not by means of the blood of goats and calves but by means of his own blood, thus securing an eternal redemption. ¹³ For if the blood of goats and bulls, and the sprinkling of defiled persons with the ashes of a heifer, sanctify for the purification of the flesh, ¹⁴ how much more will the blood of Christ, who through the eternal Spirit offered himself without blemish to God, purify our conscience from dead works to serve the living God.

¹⁹ Therefore, brothers, since we have confidence to enter the holy places by the blood of Jesus, ²⁰ by the new and living way that he opened for us through the curtain, that is, through his flesh, ²¹ and since we have a great priest over the house of God, ²² let us draw near with a true heart in full assurance of faith, with our hearts sprinkled clean from an evil conscience and our bodies washed with pure water. ²³ Let us hold fast the confession of our hope without wavering, for he who promised is faithful.

3. Read **Matthew 12:38-41** and **1 Corinthians 15:3-5.** What event in Jesus's life coincides with Jonah's time in the whale?

³⁸ Then some of the scribes and Pharisees answered him, saying,

"Teacher, we wish to see a sign from you." [39] But he answered them, "An evil and adulterous generation seeks for a sign, but no sign will be given to it except the sign of the prophet Jonah. [40] For just as Jonah was three days and three nights in the belly of the great fish, so will the Son of Man be three days and three nights in the heart of the earth. [41] The men of Nineveh will rise up at the judgment with this generation and condemn it, for they repented at the preaching of Jonah, and behold, something greater than Jonah is here.

[3] For I delivered to you as of first importance what I also received: that Christ died for our sins in accordance with the Scriptures, [4] that he was buried, that he was raised on the third day in accordance with the Scriptures, [5] and that he appeared to Cephas, then to the twelve.

Prayer/Journal Prompt:

Take some time to praise Jesus that He is...

The Lamb of God who takes away the sins of the world. When we confess our sins, God is faithful and just to forgive us because of the final substitutionary sacrifice of Christ.

The one who conquered death, spending 3 days in the earth before His resurrection, that He might be our hope for resurrection with Him.

Application and Reflection

1. God used suffering in Jonah's life to lead him back into the presence of the Lord. Read **Hebrews 12:5-13** on how God uses discipline in the life of the believer. How has God done this in your life?

> 5 And have you forgotten the exhortation that addresses you as sons?
>
> "My son, do not regard lightly the discipline of the Lord,
>
> nor be weary when reproved by him.
>
> 6 For the Lord disciplines the one he loves,
>
> and chastises every son whom he receives."
>
> 7 It is for discipline that you have to endure. God is treating you as sons. For what son is there whom his father does not discipline? 8 If you are left without discipline, in which all have participated, then you are illegitimate children and not sons. 9 Besides this, we have had earthly fathers who disciplined us and we respected them. Shall we not much more be subject to the Father of spirits and live? 10 For they disciplined us for a short time as it seemed best to them, but he disciplines us for our good, that we may share his holiness. 11 For the moment all discipline seems painful rather than pleasant, but later it yields the peaceful fruit of righteousness to those who have been trained by it.
>
> 12 Therefore lift your drooping hands and strengthen your weak knees, 13 and make straight paths for your feet, so that what is lame may not be put out of joint but rather be healed.

2. How has God proven this statement in your own life: "Salvation belongs to the Lord!" (vs. 9)?

3. In Jonah's desperation, he prayed and recalled God's words. What kinds of prayers do you pray in moments of hardship? What can you do this week to prepare to pray in light of scripture?

4. Read **Ephesians 2:1-10**.

2 And you were dead in the trespasses and sins ²in which you once walked, following the course of this world, following the prince of the power of the air, the spirit that is now at work in the sons of disobedience— ³among whom we all once lived in the passions of our flesh, carrying out the desires of the body[a] and the mind, and were by nature children of wrath, like the rest of mankind ⁴But God, being rich in mercy, because of the great love with which he loved us, ⁵even when we were dead in our trespasses, made us alive together with Christ—by grace you have been saved— ⁶and raised us up with him and seated us with him in the heavenly places in Christ Jesus, ⁷so that in the coming ages he might show the immeasurable riches of his grace in kindness toward us in Christ Jesus. ⁸For by grace you have been saved through faith. And this is not your own doing; it is the gift of God, ⁹not a result of works, so that no one may boast. ¹⁰For we are his workmanship, created in Christ Jesus for good works, which God prepared beforehand, that we should walk in them.

In what ways has God brought you from death to life?

Take some time to thank and praise God that He rescued you like He rescued Jonah.

4

God's Mercy Saves

Observation and Interpretation
Jonah 3

Read **Jonah 3** and consider the following questions.

3 Then the word of the Lord came to Jonah the second time, saying,
² "Arise, go to Nineveh, that great city, and call out against it the message that I tell you." ³ So Jonah arose and went to Nineveh, according to the word of the Lord. Now Nineveh was an exceedingly great city, three days' journey in breadth. ⁴ Jonah began to go into the city, going a day's journey. And he called out, "Yet forty days, and Nineveh shall be overthrown!" ⁵ And the people of Nineveh believed God. They called for a fast and put on sackcloth, from the greatest of them to the least of them.

⁶ The word reached the king of Nineveh, and he arose from his throne, removed his robe, covered himself with sackcloth, and sat in ashes. ⁷ And he issued a proclamation and published through Nineveh, "By the decree of the king and his nobles: Let neither man nor beast, herd nor flock, taste anything. Let them not feed or drink water, ⁸ but

let man and beast be covered with sackcloth, and let them call out mightily to God. Let everyone turn from his evil way and from the violence that is in his hands. ⁹Who knows? God may turn and relent and turn from his fierce anger, so that we may not perish."

¹⁰When God saw what they did, how they turned from their evil way, God relented of the disaster that he had said he would do to them, and he did not do it.

1. Compare Jonah 3:1-3 and Jonah 1:1-3. Describe the differences you observe in both God's call and Jonah's response.

2. Make a list of the ways the Ninevites and their King respond to Jonah's words in verses 5-6.

3. What is the proclamation of the Ninevite King in Jonah 3:7-9?

4. Describe God's response in verse 10.

Commentary

After Jonah was brought to repentance, and brought back into God's presence through prayer, he was ready to receive God's word again. Charles Spurgeon noted: "So skillful is He that with the weakest instrument he can produce the mightiest workmanship." God still used Jonah to reach the Ninevites. The result was a miraculous work of God that brought the city of Nineveh to repentance.

Verses 1-5

In a demonstration of His of redemptive and gracious generosity, God's word came to Jonah "a second time." God's second call was similar to the first one, but He said that He would give him a specific message this time. Jonah was compliant. He walked through the "great city" of Nineveh for 3 days preaching God's message.

Scholars vary in thought about what Jonah's message from God was. Some believe that Jonah literally just repeated the words of verse 4, "Yet forty days, and Nineveh shall be overthrown!" And some believe that Jonah preached about the mercy of God by telling his story of his 3 days and 3 nights in the fish.

Whatever the message was, God's words had completely equipped Jonah for the good work he was called to do (2 Timothy 3:16). Jonah merely spoke the words that God gave him and "the people of Nineveh believed God." Through His word, the "greatest and the least" of Nineveh, who before did not acknowledge the God of Israel, were brought to a deep, genuine repentance and belief that God might have mercy on them. Their changed lives displayed the power of God's word to rebellious hearts. They responded with repentance and faith, in a demonstration that "faith comes by hearing, and hearing by the word of Christ" (Romans 10:17).

Verses 6-9

The message of Jonah reached all the way up to the King, who decreed a fast throughout Nineveh. He, like the leader of the ship in Chapter 1, responded to God's impending judgment with faith that "God may turn and relent and turn from his fierce anger, so that we may not perish."

The Ninevites demonstrated a "godly sorrow leading to repentance" (2 Corinthians 7:10) that could only be a result of God's spirit at work. They wore sackcloth and ashes, which was an ancient demonstration of mourning. Their repentance and fasting, led by their king, reflects that of the repentance ordered by Israelite leaders like Esther, (Esther 4) and Jehosephat (2 Chronicles 20). God used the near-death and rescue of one Hebrew man, Jonah, to bring many Ninevites to repentance and faith in Him.

Verse 10

And when God saw what they did, how they turned from their sin, "God relented." God was eager to respond with compassion and mercy to their broken, contrite hearts.

Interpretation: Seeing Christ in Jonah Chapter 3

1. Jesus held up the Ninevites as an example of repentance in **Matthew 12:38-41**. Read this passage alongside **2 Corinthians 7:9-11**.

³⁸ Then some of the scribes and Pharisees answered him, saying, "Teacher, we wish to see a sign from you." ³⁹ But he answered them, "An evil and adulterous generation seeks for a sign, but no sign will be given to it except the sign of the prophet Jonah. ⁴⁰ For just as Jonah was three days and three nights in the belly of the great fish, so will the Son of Man be three days and three nights in the heart of the earth. ⁴¹ The men of Nineveh will rise up at the judgment with this generation and condemn it, for they repented at the preaching of Jonah, and behold, something greater than Jonah is here.

⁹ As it is, I rejoice, not because you were grieved, but because you were grieved into repenting. For you felt a godly grief, so that you suffered no loss through us.

¹⁰ For godly grief produces a repentance that leads to salvation without regret, whereas worldly grief produces death. ¹¹ For see what earnestness this godly grief has produced in you, but also what eagerness to clear yourselves, what indignation, what fear, what longing, what zeal, what punishment! At every point you have proved yourselves innocent in the matter.

Considering your observations from Jonah 3, in what ways do the Ninevites demonstrate a Godly sorrow leading to repentance?

2. Read **Matthew 12:38-41** again alongside **Matthew 16:4** and **Luke 11:29-32** and consider the following questions. ,

[38] Then some of the scribes and Pharisees answered him, saying, "Teacher, we wish to see a sign from you." [39] But he answered them, "An evil and adulterous generation seeks for a sign, but no sign will be given to it except the sign of the prophet Jonah. [40] For just as Jonah was three days and three nights in the belly of the great fish, so will the Son of Man be three days and three nights in the heart of the earth. [41] The men of Nineveh will rise up at the judgment with this generation and condemn it, for they repented at the preaching of Jonah, and behold, something greater than Jonah is here.

[4] An evil and adulterous generation seeks for a sign, but no sign will be given to it except the sign of Jonah." So he left them and departed.

[29] When the crowds were increasing, he began to say, "This generation is an evil generation. It seeks for a sign, but no sign will be given to it except the sign of Jonah. [30] For as Jonah became a sign to the people of Nineveh, so will the Son of Man be to this generation. [31] The queen of the South will rise up at the judgment with the men of this generation and condemn them, for she came from the ends of the earth to hear the wisdom of Solomon, and behold, something greater than Solomon is here. [32] The men of Nineveh will rise up at the judgment with this generation and condemn it, for they repented at the preaching of Jonah, and behold, something greater than Jonah is here.

[38] Then some of the scribes and Pharisees answered him, saying, "Teacher, we wish to see a sign from you." [39] But he answered them, "An evil and adulterous generation seeks for a sign, but no sign will be given to it except the sign of the prophet Jonah. [40] For just as Jonah was three days and three nights in the belly of the great fish, so will the Son of Man be three days and three nights in the heart of the earth. [41] The men of Nineveh will rise up at the judgment with this generation and

condemn it, for they repented at the preaching of Jonah, and behold, something greater than Jonah is here.

What do you think Jesus meant when He described the "sign of Jonah?"

How does this "sign" give us hope for our own repentance just as Jonah was the sign that led Nineveh to repentance?

3. Jonah 3 is a rare instance in the Old Testament of God sending a prophet to call non-Israelites to repentance. Read **Matthew 4:12-17** and **Ephesians 2:11-22** and consider: how does Jonah point us to Christ and the fullness of God's plan of redemption?

¹² Now when he heard that John had been arrested, he withdrew into Galilee.¹³ And leaving Nazareth he went and lived in Capernaum by the sea, in the territory of Zebulun and Naphtali, ¹⁴ so that what was spoken by the prophet Isaiah might be fulfilled:
     ¹⁵ "The land of Zebulun and the land of Naphtali,
     the way of the sea, beyond the Jordan, Galilee of the Gentiles—
¹⁶ the people dwelling in darkness
     have seen a great light,
and for those dwelling in the region and shadow of death,
     on them a light has dawned."
     ¹⁷ From that time Jesus began to preach, saying, "Repent, for the kingdom of heaven is at hand."

¹¹ Therefore remember that at one time you Gentiles in the flesh, called "the uncircumcision" by what is called the circumcision, which

is made in the flesh by hands— [12] remember that you were at that time separated from Christ, alienated from the commonwealth of Israel and strangers to the covenants of promise, having no hope and without God in the world. [13] But now in Christ Jesus you who once were far off have been brought near by the blood of Christ. [14] For he himself is our peace, who has made us both one and has broken down in his flesh the dividing wall of hostility [15] by abolishing the law of commandments expressed in ordinances, that he might create in himself one new man in place of the two, so making peace, [16] and might reconcile us both to God in one body through the cross, thereby killing the hostility. [17] And he came and preached peace to you who were far off and peace to those who were near. [18] For through him we both have access in one Spirit to the Father. [19] So then you are no longer strangers and aliens, but you are fellow citizens with the saints and members of the household of God, [20] built on the foundation of the apostles and prophets, Christ Jesus himself being the cornerstone, [21] in whom the whole structure, being joined together, grows into a holy temple in the Lord. [22] In him you also are being built together into a dwelling place for God by the Spirit.

4. The Ninevite king said, "who knows? God may turn and relent from His fierce anger..." (vs. 9) Read **John 3:16** and **1 John 1:7-10** and consider: as believers in Christ, describe how we have more certain hope that God will turn from His anger and have mercy on us?

[16] "For God so loved the world, that he gave his only Son, that whoever believes in him should not perish but have eternal life.

[7] But if we walk in the light, as he is in the light, we have fellowship with one another, and the blood of Jesus his Son cleanses us from all sin. [8] If we say we have no sin, we deceive ourselves, and the truth is not in us. [9] If we confess our sins, he is faithful and just to forgive us our

sins and to cleanse us from all unrighteousness. [10] If we say we have not sinned, we make him a liar, and his word is not in us.

Prayer/Journal Prompt

Take some time to praise Jesus that He is...

The one whom through God cleanses us from our sins, and washes us, making us "whiter than snow" that we might be restored to "the joy of our salvation." (Psalm 51)

Greater than Jonah, a sign pointing us toward repentance through His ability to overcome sin and death.

The true and better Prophet who calls people of all tribes, tongues, and nations to repentance to enter into His family.

The one who gave His life for us so that if we believe in Him, we will not perish, but God will relent of His anger toward our sin, and we will have eternal life.

Application and Reflection

1. God humbled Jonah and led him to experience repentance before he used him to call the Ninevites to repentance. Describe a time when God brought you to a place of humility in order to use you.

2. Read **Isaiah 66:1-2** and compare and contrast man's accomplishments and efforts versus what God "looks" for. How does this relate to Jonah? How does it relate to us?

Thus says the Lord:
"Heaven is my throne,
    and the earth is my footstool;
what is the house that you would build for me,
    and what is the place of my rest?
² All these things my hand has made,
    and so all these things came to be,
declares the Lord.
But this is the one to whom I will look:
    he who is humble and contrite in spirit
    and trembles at my word.

3. The Ninevites experienced a brokenness and mourning over their sin. Read **Matthew 5:4, Isaiah 66:1-2 and Psalm 51:16-17.** Reflect on how mourning over sin brings us closer to the Lord. How might this truth affect your prayer life?

[4] "Blessed are those who mourn, for they shall be comforted.

[2] All these things my hand has made,
   and so all these things came to be,
declares the Lord.
But this is the one to whom I will look:
   he who is humble and contrite in spirit
   and trembles at my word.

[16] For you will not delight in sacrifice, or I would give it;
   you will not be pleased with a burnt offering.
[17] The sacrifices of God are a broken spirit;
   a broken and contrite heart, O God, you will not despise.

5

God's Steadfast Love Endures

Observation and Interpretation
Jonah 4 and Conclusion

Read **Jonah 4** and consider the following questions.

4 But it displeased Jonah exceedingly, and he was angry. ² And he prayed to the Lord and said, "O Lord, is not this what I said when I was yet in my country? That is why I made haste to flee to Tarshish; for I knew that you are a gracious God and merciful, slow to anger and abounding in steadfast love, and relenting from disaster. ³ Therefore now, O Lord, please take my life from me, for it is better for me to die than to live." ⁴ And the Lord said, "Do you do well to be angry?"

⁵ Jonah went out of the city and sat to the east of the city and made a booth for himself there. He sat under it in the shade, till he should see what would become of the city. ⁶ Now the Lord God appointed a plant and made it come up over Jonah, that it might be a shade over his head, to save him from his discomfort. So Jonah was exceedingly glad because of the plant. ⁷ But when dawn came up the next day, God appointed a worm that attacked the plant, so that it withered. ⁸ When

the sun rose, God appointed a scorching east wind, and the sun beat down on the head of Jonah so that he was faint. And he asked that he might die and said, "It is better for me to die than to live." ⁹ But God said to Jonah, "Do you do well to be angry for the plant?" And he said, "Yes, I do well to be angry, angry enough to die." ¹⁰ And the Lord said, "You pity the plant, for which you did not labor, nor did you make it grow, which came into being in a night and perished in a night. ¹¹ And should not I pity Nineveh, that great city, in which there are more than 120,000 persons who do not know their right hand from their left, and also much cattle?"

1. Describe Jonah's reaction to God's mercy in verses 1-5.

2. What do you think Jonah's reaction reveals about his heart for God's mission?

3. Read **Deuteronomy 7:6-8** and consider the following questions.

⁶ "For you are a people holy to the Lord your God. The Lord your God has chosen you to be a people for his treasured possession, out of all the peoples who are on the face of the earth. ⁷ It was not because you were more in number than any other people that the Lord set his love on you and chose you, for you were the fewest of all peoples, ⁸ but it is because the Lord loves you and is keeping the oath that he swore to your fathers, that the Lord has brought you out with a mighty hand and redeemed you from the house of slavery, from the hand of Pharaoh king of Egypt.

According to Deuteronomy 7, on what basis did God choose the people that Jonah represents?

Considering this, does Jonah "have a right" (NIV) to be angry about God having mercy on Nineveh?

4. In verses 5-11 God cares for Jonah in his distress, and at the same time, creates a parable for him. Fill out this chart to help you understand God's lesson for Jonah.

The Plant's creation and de-struction:	Jonah's heart and response:
Nineveh's creation in God's image, and their repentance:	God's heart and response:

5. What is God's question and challenge for Jonah in verses 9-11?

Why do you think the book ends this way?

Commentary

In Chapter 3, Jonah was finally compliant to God's commands. But in Chapter 4, it is revealed that though Jonah had outwardly obeyed God, his heart was not in line with God's gracious plan. As we conclude we see that Jonah was just like us, and just like every other prophet and child of God throughout history; Jonah still had a lot to learn about God. (Begg, Man Overboard). As Jonah wrestled with God and His word, God continued to pursue him with patience, grace, and compassion.

Verses 1-4

Jonah was "displeased...exceedingly" at God's mercy toward the Ninevites. This reaction might surprise us. We would assume that Jonah would be humbled and overjoyed that God would use him to bring an entire city to repentance. But his heart is revealed in the second verse, and we receive insight into Jonah's fleeing in Chapter 1. "Is not this what I said when I was in my country..." Jonah explained to God that God's compassion for the Ninevites was what he was afraid of. God's mercy was the reason Jonah didn't want to go to Nineveh.

Jonah was wrestling with the real-life implications of God's gracious character. In doing so, he quoted God's description of Himself as stated in Exodus 34:6. "I knew that you are a gracious God, and merciful, slow to anger, and abounding in steadfast love." Jonah speaks God's word back to God, but he uses it as an accusation as he vents and complains. When he experienced God's great compassion toward Nineveh, Jonah was so angry and depressed he would rather not be alive.

The NIV translates God's responding question, "Have you any right to be angry?" Jonah had received saving grace and mercy when he was cast into the sea, and it caused him to "rejoice" in the God of "steadfast love." But when this same grace was extended to others, it made Jonah "exceedingly" angry. Jonah's misunderstanding of grace and of his people's identity and purpose is revealed here. Somewhere along the way, Jonah thought he had earned God's grace. Jonah was still wrestling with the reality that "salvation is from the Lord." (Jonah 2:9). He had no right to be angry.

Verse 5

As Jonah hung on to the hope that God might still destroy the city and that the mission might go according to Jonah's plan, he "went out of the city and sat to the east of the city." He made a booth and watched to see what would become of Nineveh.

Verses 6-10

Jonah angrily watched the city, and God graciously provided a vine to shade him from the heat. Depending on the translation, it is called a vine, a plant, or a gourd. Jonah had been stripped of his loves and purposes, and he was grasping onto anything for hope and comfort at this point; the gift of the plant masks Jonah's anger for a while. Verse 6 says he went from being "exceedingly" displeased at his ruined plans to "exceedingly" happy at the sight of the plant. Jonah's drastic change in emotion and devotion is telling. Lacking a secure foundation in God makes us susceptible to loving things like vines, comfort, and ministry success more than God and His grace. The Bible calls this idolatry.

God takes away the plant the next day by appointing a worm to attack it. Then He appoints a scorching east wind. God was disciplining Jonah through this mini-parable to protect him. Just like God "appointed" the storm and the whale, God appointed the vine and the worm in order to bring Jonah back into His presence. God pursued him and rescued him, yet again, from a life centered on a hope other than God's grace.

John Newton wrote a hymn on this event in Jonah 4 entitled, "I Asked the Lord that I Might Grow..."

I asked the Lord that I might grow
In faith, and love, and every grace;
Might more of His salvation know,
And seek, more earnestly, His face.

"Twas He who taught me thus to pray,
And He, I trust, has answered prayer!
But it has been in such a way,
As almost drove me to despair.

I hoped that in some favored hour,
At once He'd answer my request;
And by His love's constraining pow'r,
Subdue my sins, and give me rest.

Instead of this, He made me feel
The hidden evils of my heart;
And let the angry pow'rs of hell
Assault my soul in every part.

Yea more, with His own hand He seemed
Intent to aggravate my woe;
Crossed all the fair designs I schemed,
Blasted my gourds, and laid me low.

Lord, why is this, I trembling cried,
Wilt thou pursue thy worm to death?
"'Tis in this way, the Lord replied,
I answer prayer for grace and faith.

These inward trials I employ,
From self, and pride, to set thee free;
And break thy schemes of earthly joy,
That thou may'st find thy all in Me."

The "hidden evils" and empty hopes of Jonah's heart had been revealed-
he hoped that the pagans outside of God's chosen people, Israel,
would perish for their sins. He hoped in a comfortable, reputable, tidy
ministry where the outwardly righteous were blessed and sinners were
destroyed. Tim Keller eloquently said, "God 'blasted his gourds,' not
just the literal one that had given him shade and comfort but also the
bigger one, his passion for his nation's prosperity and success, and his
biggest one, his pride in his own righteousness." (Rediscovering, 223).
God's heart and plan of grace had been exalted higher than Jonah's
plans. God had received all the glory in spite of Jonah, and Jonah was
left exposed as full of pride, self-righteousness, and idolatry.

God continued to patiently pursue Jonah's heart. He gave him another
chance to evaluate his response, "Do you do well to be angry for the
plant?" Jonah explained that yes, "he does well to be angry," in fact
angry enough to die. Then God used the illustration of the plant to
teach him about His compassion.

Jonah had compassion for the plant- but Jonah did not raise up the
plant, work for, or water the plant. The plant only lasted one day, but
when the plant perished, Jonah was distressed enough to die.

God gently pursued Jonah at his level as He explained: if Jonah cared for
the plant, how much more should God care for Nineveh? God's heart
was and is for all the nations, including those 120,000 persons made in
His own image, that they might receive His steadfast love and mercy.
God cared about Nineveh. The story ends as the writer gives God the
glory for His great compassion, stating His final question to Jonah,
"Should I not pity Nineveh, that great city...?" Jonah ended this event

in his life as one deeply humbled, and in ending his story with God's question, God gets the glory for His gracious heart.

God's pursuit of His people throughout Jonah demonstrates that the hearts of both his servants, and those they serve are of infinite importance to Him. He pursued Jonah, the mariners at Joppa, and the people of Nineveh, demonstrating His rescuing grace and compassion. Through Christ, we are the recipients of this pursuit, too.

Hebrews 1:1 says, "Long ago, at many times and in many ways, God spoke to our fathers by the prophets, but in these last days he has spoken to us by his Son." Centuries after Jonah's ministry, God's compassion, undeserved mercy, and heart for all nations was fully revealed through His word made flesh, Jesus Christ. Christ's apostle Peter wrote to a dispersed church consisting of many different nations and ethnicities; he explained how to receive and extend the grace of God.

"But you are a chosen race, a royal priesthood, a holy nation, a people for his own possession, that you may proclaim the excellencies of him who called you out of darkness into his marvelous light. Once you were not a people, but now you are God's people; once you had not received mercy, but now you have received mercy." 1 Peter 2:9-10

If we have received His mercy, we are to extend it to others as we proclaim His light and excellence. It is for this purpose we have been saved! We, like Jonah, need God's great mercy and grace that we might receive His word, behold and treasure His heart above all else, and with Christ-like love, serve those made in His image, "to the praise of His glorious grace." (Ephesians 1:6)

Interpretation: Seeing Christ in Jonah 4

1. Read **Luke 15:11-32** and consider the following questions.

¹¹ And he said, "There was a man who had two sons. ¹² And the younger of them said to his father, 'Father, give me the share of property that is coming to me.' And he divided his property between them. ¹³ Not many days later, the younger son gathered all he had and took a journey into a far country, and there he squandered his property in reckless living. ¹⁴ And when he had spent everything, a severe famine arose in that country, and he began to be in need. ¹⁵ So he went and hired himself out to one of the citizens of that country, who sent him into his fields to feed pigs. ¹⁶ And he was longing to be fed with the pods that the pigs ate, and no one gave him anything.

¹⁷ "But when he came to himself, he said, 'How many of my father's hired servants have more than enough bread, but I perish here with hunger! ¹⁸ I will arise and go to my father, and I will say to him, "Father, I have sinned against heaven and before you. ¹⁹ I am no longer worthy to be called your son. Treat me as one of your hired servants."' ²⁰ And he arose and came to his father. But while he was still a long way off, his father saw him and felt compassion, and ran and embraced him and kissed him. ²¹ And the son said to him, 'Father, I have sinned against heaven and before you. I am no longer worthy to be called your son.' ²² But the father said to his servants, 'Bring quickly the best robe, and put it on him, and put a ring on his hand, and shoes on his feet. ²³ And bring the fattened calf and kill it, and let us eat and celebrate. ²⁴ For this my son was dead, and is alive again; he was lost, and is found.' And they began to celebrate.

²⁵ "Now his older son was in the field, and as he came and drew

near to the house, he heard music and dancing. [26] And he called one of the servants and asked what these things meant. [27] And he said to him, 'Your brother has come, and your father has killed the fattened calf, because he has received him back safe and sound.'[28] But he was angry and refused to go in. His father came out and entreated him,[29] but he answered his father, 'Look, these many years I have served you, and I never disobeyed your command, yet you never gave me a young goat, that I might celebrate with my friends. [30] But when this son of yours came, who has devoured your property with prostitutes, you killed the fattened calf for him!' [31] And he said to him, 'Son, you are always with me, and all that is mine is yours. [32] It was fitting to celebrate and be glad, for this your brother was dead, and is alive; he was lost, and is found.'"

In Jonah 1-2, how does Jonah act like the younger son? In Jonah 4, how does he act like the older son?

2. What similarities do you see between the response of the father in Luke 15:11-32 and God in Jonah 1-4?

What does this tell you about God's character toward His struggling children?

3. Re-read about God's view of sinners in Jonah 4:10-11, and other descriptions of this perspective in **Genesis 6:6, Isaiah 63:9** and **Matthew 9:36.** How does God's view of rebellious people reflect His compassion and generosity?

⁶ And the Lord regretted that he had made man on the earth, and it grieved him to his heart.

⁹ In all their affliction he was afflicted,
  and the angel of his presence saved them;
in his love and in his pity he redeemed them;
  he lifted them up and carried them all the days of old.

³⁶ When he saw the crowds, he had compassion for them, because they were harassed and helpless, like sheep without a shepherd.

4. Tim Keller says that Jesus is the "weeping God of Jonah 4 in human form" (Rediscovering, 123). Read **Luke 13:34, 22:40-46,** and **23:32-43.** How is this so?

³⁴ O Jerusalem, Jerusalem, the city that kills the prophets and stones those who are sent to it! How often would I have gathered your children together as a hen gathers her brood under her wings, and you were not willing!

⁴⁰ And when he came to the place, he said to them, "Pray that you may not enter into temptation." ⁴¹ And he withdrew from them about a stone's throw, and knelt down and prayed, ⁴² saying, "Father, if you are willing, remove this cup from me. Nevertheless, not my will, but yours, be done." ⁴³ And there appeared to him an angel from heaven, strengthening him. ⁴⁴ And being in agony he prayed more earnestly;

and his sweat became like great drops of blood falling down to the ground. [45] And when he rose from prayer, he came to the disciples and found them sleeping for sorrow, [46] and he said to them, "Why are you sleeping? Rise and pray that you may not enter into temptation."

[32] Two others, who were criminals, were led away to be put to death with him. [33] And when they came to the place that is called The Skull, there they crucified him, and the criminals, one on his right and one on his left. [34] And Jesus said, "Father, forgive them, for they know not what they do." And they cast lots to divide his garments. [35] And the people stood by, watching, but the rulers scoffed at him, saying, "He saved others; let him save himself, if he is the Christ of God, his Chosen One!" [36] The soldiers also mocked him, coming up and offering him sour wine [37] and saying, "If you are the King of the Jews, save yourself!" [38] There was also an inscription over him, "This is the King of the Jews."

[39] One of the criminals who were hanged railed at him, saying, "Are you not the Christ? Save yourself and us!" [40] But the other rebuked him, saying, "Do you not fear God, since you are under the same sentence of condemnation? [41] And we indeed justly, for we are receiving the due reward of our deeds; but this man has done nothing wrong." [42] And he said, "Jesus, remember me when you come into your kingdom." [43] And he said to him, "Truly, I say to you, today you will be with me in paradise."

Prayer/Journal Prompt

Take some time to praise Jesus that He is...

The one through whom both the older and younger prodigal child can come to their Father, knowing that He will receive them with mercy, grace and steadfast love.

The One who did not come to condemn the world, but to save those who are "harassed and helpless" like sheep without a shepherd (Matthew 9:36).

The One who loves His enemies and prays for those who persecute Him. And the One who died for us while we were His enemies that we might be reconciled to God.

Application and Reflection

1. How are you like Jonah in his "younger brother" tendencies? How are you like him in his "older brother" tendencies?

2. How have you seen God's compassion toward you in both your younger and older brother tendencies?

3. Read **Romans 5:10-11** and **Ephesians 2:1-22** and consider the following questions.

¹⁰ For if while we were enemies we were reconciled to God by the death of his Son, much more, now that we are reconciled, shall we be saved by his life. ¹¹ More than that, we also rejoice in God through our Lord Jesus Christ, through whom we have now received reconciliation.

2 And you were dead in the trespasses and sins ² in which you once walked, following the course of this world, following the prince of the power of the air, the spirit that is now at work in the sons of disobedience— ³ among whom we all once lived in the passions of our flesh, carrying out the desires of the body and the mind, and were by nature children of wrath, like the rest of mankind. ⁴ But God, being rich in

mercy, because of the great love with which he loved us, ⁵even when we were dead in our trespasses, made us alive together with Christ—by grace you have been saved— ⁶and raised us up with him and seated us with him in the heavenly places in Christ Jesus, ⁷so that in the coming ages he might show the immeasurable riches of his grace in kindness toward us in Christ Jesus. ⁸For by grace you have been saved through faith. And this is not your own doing; it is the gift of God, ⁹not a result of works, so that no one may boast. ¹⁰For we are his workmanship, created in Christ Jesus for good works, which God prepared beforehand, that we should walk in them.

¹¹Therefore remember that at one time you Gentiles in the flesh, called "the uncircumcision" by what is called the circumcision, which is made in the flesh by hands— ¹²remember that you were at that time separated from Christ, alienated from the commonwealth of Israel and strangers to the covenants of promise, having no hope and without God in the world. ¹³But now in Christ Jesus you who once were far off have been brought near by the blood of Christ. ¹⁴For he himself is our peace, who has made us both one and has broken down in his flesh the dividing wall of hostility ¹⁵by abolishing the law of commandments expressed in ordinances, that he might create in himself one new man in place of the two, so making peace, ¹⁶and might reconcile us both to God in one body through the cross, thereby killing the hostility. ¹⁷And he came and preached peace to you who were far off and peace to those who were near. ¹⁸For through him we both have access in one Spirit to the Father. ¹⁹So then you are no longer strangers and aliens, but you are fellow citizens with the saints and members of the household of God, ²⁰built on the foundation of the apostles and prophets, Christ Jesus himself being the cornerstone, ²¹in whom the whole structure, being joined together, grows into a holy temple in the Lord. ²²In him you also are being built together into a dwelling place for God by the Spirit.

How does the nature of how we are saved (Romans 5:10-11 and Ephesians 2:1-10) inform the way we view being united with others different than ourselves? (Ephesians 2:11-22)

How is this truth personal to you and your circumstances?

4. What have you learned about the difference between where Jonah put his hope, and our true hope in the grace of Christ?

How will our true hope in Christ encourage you to live "for the praise of His glorious grace?" (Ephesians 1:6)

Bibliography

1. Citations marked "ESV Study Bible" are taken from the ESV® Study Bible (The Holy Bible, English Standard Version®), copyright ©2008 by Crossway, a publishing ministry of Good News Publishers. Used by permission. All rights reserved.
2. Unless otherwise noted, scripture quotations are from the ESV® Bible (The Holy Bible, English Standard Version®), © 2001 by Crossway, a publishing ministry of Good News Publishers. Used by permission. All rights reserved. The ESV text may not be quoted in any publication made available to the public by a Creative Commons license. The ESV may not be translated in whole or in part into any other language. The Holy Bible, English Standard Version®, is adapted from the Revised Standard Version of the Bible, copyright Division of Christian Education of the National Council of the Churches of Christ in the U.S.A."
3. Scripture quotations marked (NIV) are taken from the Holy Bible, New International Version®, NIV®. Copyright © 1973, 1978, 1984, 2011 by Biblica, Inc.™ Used by permission of Zondervan. All rights reserved worldwide. www.zondervan.comThe "NIV" and "New International Version" are trademarks registered in the United States Patent and Trademark Office by Biblica, Inc.™
4. Akin, Daniel. "Christocentric Hermeneutics." Hermeneutics, Southeastern Baptist Theological Seminary. Lecture handout.
5. Begg, Allistar. Sermons from the Book of Jonah. Truth for Life: The Bible Teaching Ministry of Allistar Begg. October 1, 2019. https://blog.truthforlife.org/sermons-from-jonah-by-alistair-begg
6. Guthrie, Nancy. (2021, January 21). Collin Smith on Jonah (No. 127) *Help Me Teach the Bible*. The Gospel Coalition. https://www.thegospelcoalition.org/podcasts/help-me-teach-the-bible/colin-smith-on-jonah/
7. Keller, Tim. Rediscovering Jonah. Copyright 2018 by Timothy Keller. New York, New York. Viking, an imprint of Penguin Random House, 2018
8. Newton, John. "I Asked the Lord that I Might Grow" *The Trinity Psalter Hymnal*, 2018, p. 790. *org*, https://hymnary.org/text/i_asked_the_lord_that_i_might_grow
9. Sinclair Ferguson, *Man Overboard: The Story of Jonah*, Edinburgh: Banner of Truth Trust, 2008.

10. Spurgeon, Charles Haddon. "Commentary on Jonah". "Spurgeon's Verse Expositions of the Bible". https://www.studylight.org/commentaries/eng/spe/jonah-1.html. 2011.

11. Spurgeon, Charles Haddon. "What Meanest Thou O Sleeper?" https://www.spurgeon.org/resource-library/scripture-index/jonah/